HOW DO I START RESCUING THE WORLD WITH THIS BOOK?

 1 ASK A GROWN-UP TO GET THE CARS OFF THE BOOK. TRY SCISSORS.

2 FOLD OUT THE ROAD PAGES AND START ROLLING!

TIP Extend the roads by drawing your own. Where else can you find to drive? Maybe there's an emergency in Dad's shoe!

ADD YOUR OWN STUFF TO THE ROAD PAGES

TIP Pretend that blocks are buildings.

TIP Clay makes good mud. You can add rocks, too.

Use your imagination to create amazing obstacles and hazards for your trucks using stuff you can find around the house.

woooooooooooooooooooooo

ALIENS ATTACK CITY!

Oh no! Spaceships have landed in the city and silly aliens are causing all sorts of trouble! Hellllppp!

OTHER COOL IDEAS:

- Tape a square of paper to a flat toothpick to make a flagpole.
- Make buildings with boxes, blocks, and LEGOS.™
- Silly Putty® or Slime looks like a gooky toxic spill.
- Cut-up new sponges look like building bricks. Use the snowplow to shovel them out of the road.

TIP Tissue paper makes great fire.

CROC
x-ing

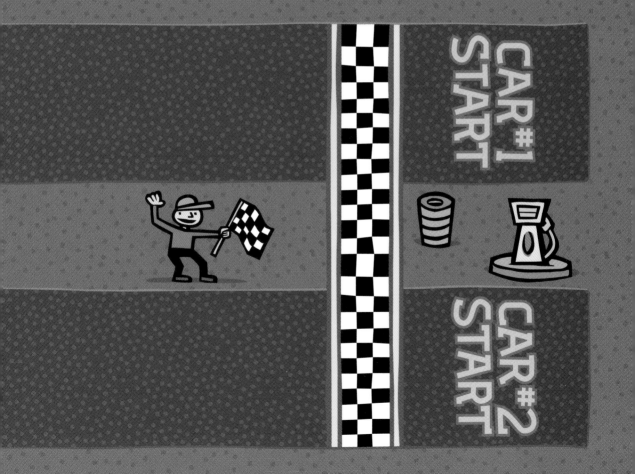

CAR #1 START

CAR #2 START

FALLING ROCKS

FIND THESE CARS AND RESCUE THE DRIVERS BEFORE THE RACE IS OVER!

SWAMP RACE

Professional car racing can be dangerous! How fast can you race around the slippery track and rescue the drivers?

YIKES! They're going to crash!

TIP Your toy animals can play, too.

TIP Make a bridge from a paper towel roll. Add twigs and rocks to make the scene extra swampy.

RESCUE RACERS

SETTING UP

Prop this book open over some blocks, cushions, stuffed animals or a pile of books. See what works best.

COLLISION COURSE!

Set up ramps and obstacles for more action. Try racing the trucks over the edge of a table.

HOW TO RACE

Line your trucks up at the top of the race page and let 'em rip! Whichever truck rolls the farthest wins.

OBSTACLES

All sorts of things can block the path of your raceway — other trucks, toys or even Mom's foot!

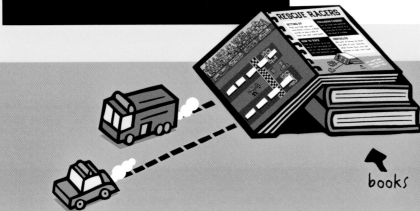

books

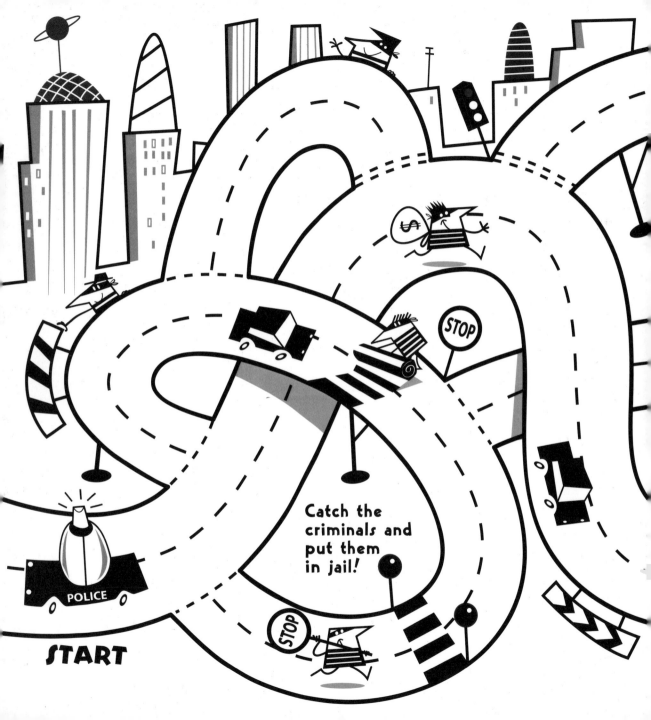

Catch the criminals and put them in jail!

STOP

POLICE

START

IT'S A JUNGLE

Even animals need help sometimes. A sleeping rhino is blocking the road. What other animals do you see that need rescuing?

GULP!

Find your favorite pens or crayons...

It's a BLIZZARD

Snow days are fun, but not when you're stuck inside your house. It's been snowing for days and days. Can you help clear the roads?

TIP Cotton balls make great pretend snow.

TIP Add tiny toy trees to the scene. And if a tree falls down? The snowplow can help move it!

brrr!

...and paint the
rescue trucks!

MORE FUN BOOKS FROM

Chicken Socks

Castle	Highlight This Book!
The Superhero Starter Kit	How to Make Pompom Animals
Magic Painting	Hand Art
Amazing Lacing	Shadow Games
Pop Bead Critters	How To Tell Time
Foam Gliders	The Super Scissors Book
Tree House Bugs	Tricky Stickies